Paul Outerbridge Jr.

Paul Outerbridge Jr., der 1896 in New York geboren wurde und 1958 in Kalifornien starb, war Designer und Illustrator, bevor er zu Beginn der 20er Jahre Photograph wurde. Im Jahr 1925 ging er nach Paris, wo er für die französische *Vogue* arbeitete und bald zum Freundeskreis um Picasso, Man Ray, Duchamp und Strawinsky gehörte. Aus dieser Zeit stammen seine Mode- und Sachaufnahmen, die ihn als Perfektionisten mit höchsten technischen und ästhetischen Ansprüchen sowie als den eigentlichen Repräsentanten der kubistisch-abstrakten Photographie ausweisen.

Um 1930 wandte sich Outerbridge dann – auf der Suche nach neuen, reizvollen Herausforderungen – der Farbphotographie zu, insbesondere der Entwicklung des ebenso komplizierten wie aufwendigen »Carbro-Color«-Verfahrens. Mit Hilfe ausgefeilter Techniken und beflügelt von bilderstürmerischer Phantasie entstand seine Serie erotischer Frauenbildnisse, deren fetischistischer Charakter unübersehbar ist. Der beunruhigende Realismus dieser farbigen Aufnahmen veranlaßte sei-nerzeit Museumsdirektoren, Kritiker und Verleger, sich von Outerbridges Schaffen zu distanzieren.

Der vorliegende Band versammelt siebenundvierzig der wichtigsten Aufnahmen von Paul Outerbridge, dessen Rang als einer der großen Photographen unseres Jahrhunderts heute unbestritten ist. Den einleitenden Essay verfaßte die Kunsthistorikerin Jeannine Fiedler.

Paul Outerbridge Jr., who was born in New York in 1896 and died in California in 1958, was a designer and illustrator before he turned to photography at the beginning of the 1920s. In 1925 he moved to Paris, where he worked for the French edition of *Vogue* and soon joined a circle of friends including Picasso, Man Ray, Duchamp, and Stravinsky. His fashion and still-life photographs date from this period, and show him to be a perfectionist with the highest possible technical and aesthetic standards and a genuine representative of Cubist and abstract photography.

Around 1930, looking for new, more interesting challenges, Outerbridge turned to color photography, and particularly to the development of the "carbro-color" process, which was both complex and time-consuming. Using sophisticated techniques, and inspired by his iconoclastic fantasy, he produced a series of erotic female portraits whose fetishistic quality is unmistakable. The disturbing realism of these color images caused museum directors, critics, and publishers of the period to distance themselves from him.

Paul Outerbridge's status as one of the great photographers of our century is today undisputed, and the present volume gathers together forty-seven of the most important of his photographs.

The introductory essay is by the art historian Jeannine Fiedler.

96 Seiten, 47 Tafeln in Farbe und Duotone
Deutsch/englische Ausgabe

96 pages, 47 illustrations in color and duotone
German/English edition

Paul Outerbridge Jr.

Photographien / Photographs

Mit einem Text von / with a text by

Jeannine Fiedler

Schirmer/Mosel

MÜNCHEN · PARIS · LONDON

Bildnachweis / Picture Credits:
G. Ray Hawkins Gallery, Santa Monica, California: Tafeln / plates 2, 11, 13,
18, 22, 25, 26, 42, 44, 46, Rückentitel / back cover;
Laguna Art Museum, Laguna Beach, California: Tafeln / plates 1, 5, 15, 17, 19, 32;
Graham Howe, Pasadena, California: Tafeln / plates 6, 7, 14, 21, 40;
Robert Miller Gallery, New York: Tafeln / plates 29, 35, 45;
The Library of Congress, Washington, D. C.: Tafeln / plates 3, 4;
The Cleveland Museum of Art, Cleveland, Ohio: Tafel / plate 41.

Abbildungen auf dem Umschlag / Illustrations on the cover:
Paul Outerbridge Jr., *›Phoenix Rising‹*, 1937 (Titel / front cover)
Paul Outerbridge Jr., *Toilet Paper Advertisement*, ca. 1938 (Rückentitel / back cover)

Translation from the German by Michael Robertson

Die Deutsche Bibliothek – CIP-Einheitsaufnahme
Outerbridge, Paul:
Paul Outerbridge jr., Photographien / Mit einem Text von Jeannine Fiedler. –
München ; Paris ; London : Schirmer-Mosel, 1996
Beitr. dt. und engl.
ISBN 3-88814-811-1
NE: Fiedler, Jeannine [Mitarb.]; HST

A CIP catalogue record for this book
is available from the British Library.

Printed in Italy by EBS, Verona
ISBN 3-88814-811-1

Eine Schirmer/Mosel Produktion
A Schirmer/Mosel Production

Dompteur der Weiblichkeit / Tamer of Femininity

Jeannine Fiedler

Nur wenige photographische Œuvres der klassischen modernen Periode unseres Jahrhunderts zeichnen sich durch eine solch kontinuierliche stilistische Eleganz aus. Und nur wenigen Photographen gelang in den noch jungen Farbverfahren nach hundert Jahren der Schwarzweiß-Photographie der Übergang oder auch nur der Versuch zu einer neuen aufregenden Farbästhetik. Paul Outerbridge, von dessen Arbeiten hier die Rede sein soll, ist dennoch vielen, die dem Medium Photographie aufgeschlossen gegenüberstehen, ein Unbekannter. Dies mag daher rühren, daß seinen Photographien jegliches spekulative Moment fremd ist. Wohl spielt Outerbridge mit den Phantasien der Betrachter, können sich Dialoge zwischen ihnen und Outerbridges Modellen entzünden, leitet er sein Publikum in magische Objektwelten. Doch stets ist die Kadrage seiner Kamera ausgefüllt mit Arrangements von Gegenständen oder vorzugsweise weiblichen Modellen, durchkomponiert bis ins letzte Detail, durchdrungen von einem Willen zu einer vollkommen durchgestalteten Ästhetik. Dem Zufall wird in seinen Arbeiten die Tür gewiesen. Die künstlerische Leichtigkeit eines Man Ray, der durch ein Versehen in der Dunkelkammer die Photogrammtechnik wiederentdeckte, oder den Bildwitz eines an phototechnischen Problemen völlig desinteressierten Laszlo Moholy-Nagy sucht man in Outerbridges Werk vergeblich. Der verspätete Bohemien Outerbridge flaniert in seinen »künstlichen Paradiesen«, beobachtet und arrangiert akribisch genau den Kosmos der Dinge und der Weiblichkeit und frönt seinem extravaganten Perfektionismus.

Die üblichen Lektionen eines Künstlerlebens in Armut und Exzeß wurden dem aus großbürgerlichem Hause stammenden Outerbridge geschenkt. »Fünf Jahre nachdem mein Vater, ein bedeutender Arzt aus einer angesehenen Familie aus Bermuda, meine Mutter, eine Frau ohne gesellschaftliche Stellung, aber aus der ganz ordentlichen Familie eines Geistlichen, geheiratet hatte, wurde ich in 35 West in der 53. Straße geboren.«[1] Das war im Jahre 1896 in New York City. Statt auf väterliche Bitten hin vier weitere Jahre an Allgemeinwissen an der Harvard University aufzunehmen, entschloß sich Outerbridge nach einer Kindheit und Jugend »als richtiges Mutter-

Few of the photographic oeuvres of this century's classical modernist period show comparable continuity in their stylistic elegance. And during the early years of color processing, few photographers succeeded, after a hundred years of black-and-white photography, in making the transition to a new and exciting aesthetics of color, or even attempted it. Paul Outerbridge achieved both of these feats, but has nevertheless remained unknown to many who are interested in the medium of photography. Possibly this is because there is nothing speculative about his photographs. He toys with the observer's fantasies, it is possible for dialogue to arise between the observer and Outerbridge's models, and he leads his public into worlds full of magical objects. But the center of the camera's image, filled with arrangements of objects or preferably with female models, is always totally composed down to the last detail, and shaped by an ambition to achieve a perfectly structured aesthetics. Nothing is left to chance in these works. One looks in vain in Outerbridge's photography for the light artistic touch of a Man Ray, who rediscovered the technique of the photogram as a result of an accident in the darkroom, or the photographic sense of humor of Laszlo Moholy-Nagy, who was quite uninterested in the technical problems of photography. Outerbridge, a late bohemian, saunters through his "artifical paradises," observes and arranges a cosmos of objects and femininity with meticulous exactness, and indulges his own extravagant perfectionism.

Outerbridge, who came from a well-off family, was spared the usual lessons in poverty and excess that artists undergo in the course of their careers. "Five years after my father, an important doctor from a respected family in Bermuda, married my mother, a woman of no standing in society but from the quite acceptable family of a minister of religion, I was born in 35 West 53rd Street."[1] It was in 1896 in New York City. After a childhood and youth spent as a "real mother's little boy," Outerbridge decided on an artistic training instead of continuing with four more years of general education at Harvard University, as his father would have preferred. He studied portrait and nude painting at the Art Students' League in New York. At the age of eighteen he wrote a revue

söhnchen« zu einer künstlerischen Ausbildung. Er studierte Portrait- und Aktzeichnen an der Art Students' League in New York. Mit achtzehn Jahren schrieb er eine Revue, bei der er sein eigener Kostüm- und Bühnenbildner, Szenarist und Produzent war. Die Show, die Geld für ein Kontingent britischer Truppen in Übersee im gerade einsetzenden Ersten Weltkrieg einbringen sollte, wurde ein großer Erfolg. Im selben Jahr begann er mit der Gestaltung von Plakaten, auf einigen von ihnen die ersten »Modernen«, die in den Vereinigten Staaten vorgestellt wurden. Ein neues Atelier in Greenwich Village führte den jungen Paul Outerbridge ins Herz der New Yorker Künstlerszene und in die Nähe Marcel Duchamps, der Outerbridges photographische Arbeiten später sehr schätzen sollte. Seine freiwillige Meldung als Pilot beim Royal Flying Corps, 1917, mündete in eine Phase der Entfremdung und physischen Überbelastung, die ihn zu einer Bestandsaufnahme seines bisherigen Lebens zwang. Auf der Suche nach einer zukünftigen Ausrichtung seiner Existenz lernte er Paula Smith, eine junge Frau aus begüterter Familie, kennen. Die beiden heirateten 1921, und eine jährliche Apanage befreite die Ehe von finanziellen Sorgen.

Outerbridge, den bislang nichts so recht zu fesseln vermochte, entdeckte in jenem Sommer eine besondere Affinität zur Photographie, die er an der Clarence H. White School auszuloten begann. »Ich hatte ziemlich viel als Amateur mit der Photographie herumexperimentiert und irgendwie kam mir die Idee, das als Geschäft zu betreiben. Im Herbst fing ich an, ernsthaft zu studieren, und belegte einen Kurs an der Schule.«[2] Dem Piktorialismus, zu dessen Hauptexponenten White vormals gehörte, hatten die Studierenden längst abgeschworen. Beflügelt von einer neuen, direkten und dem Medium adäquateren Art, die Dinge zu sehen und zu photographieren, orientierte man sich am Kubismus und setzte sich in der Abstraktion mit den plastischen Formen der Gegenstände auseinander. Outerbridge verspürte hier eine wahre Inspiration und den »vitalen Impuls zur Arbeit«. In jener Zeit entstanden seine ersten Stilleben: sensible Studien komplexer Licht- und Schattenverhältnisse in Kompositionen mit Schachteln, Schüsseln, Vasen und seine berühmten Untersuchungen der Form des Eies. Während sich diese frühen Stilleben, seine urbanen Impressionen von Manhattan und auch die ersten zarten Akte – ausschnitthafte, abstrahierte Torsi – noch durch ein warmes inneres Leuchten auf körnigen Platindrucken stimmungsvoll verdichten, strahlt auf den Werbeaufnahmen von Textilien und Schmuck schon der kühle Glanz der späteren Farbaufnahmen.

Für Outerbridges Schwarzweiß-Photographie wie für die gesamte Sachphotographie bis hin zur Neuen Sachlichkeit in

in which he was his own costume and stage designer, writer, and producer. The show, which was staged to collect money for the British Expeditionary Force at the beginning of the First World War, was an immense success. In the same year he started designing posters, some of them for the first "Modernists" who were shown at galleries in the United States. A new studio in Greenwich Village put the young Outerbridge at the heart of the New York art scene and in contact with Marcel Duchamp, who was later to have a high opinion of Outerbridge's photographic work. Outerbridge volunteered for service with the Royal Flying Corps in 1917, and entered a phase of alienation and physical overexertion that made it necessary for him to re-evaluate his life. As he was searching for direction for the future, he met Paula Smith, a young woman from a well-to-do family. They married in 1921, and a considerable annual allowance freed them from financial worries.

That summer, Outerbridge, whose attention and interests had so far not been gripped by any one field in particular, discovered his special affinity for photography. He began to explore it at the Clarence H. White School of Photography at Columbia University. "I had experimented with photography quite a lot as an amateur and the idea somehow came to me that I could do it as a business. In the fall I started serious studies and took a college course."[2] The students had long since abandoned pictorialism, of which White had formerly been a principal exponent. Inspired by a new, direct way of seeing and photographing things that was more appropriate to the medium, they were orienting themselves around Cubism and exploring the sculptural shapes of objects in abstraction. Outerbridge found his true inspiration here, and a "vital impulse to work." During this period his first still lifes were produced: sensitive studies in complex light and shadow conditions with compositions of cartons, bowls, vases, and his famous explorations of the shape of the egg. These early still lifes, urban impressions of Manhattan as well as early, delicate nudes – cutout-like, abstract torsos – are still atmospheric and dense, with a warm, inner glow on grainy platinum prints; but the advertising shots of textiles and jewelry already have the cool brilliance of the later color photographs.

Causal connections between things were unimportant not only in Outerbridge's black-and-white photography but also in still-life photography in general, even down to the Neue Sachlichkeit movement in Europe. It was not relationships between objects that were interesting, but the things themselves, their essences, that were being analyzed. In 1922, Outerbridge created one of the icons of this photographic

Europa waren die kausalen Zusammenhänge zwischen den Dingen unwichtig. Nicht die Beziehungen wollte man kennenlernen, sondern gerade die Sachen selbst, ihre Essenz, ihr Wesen wurden hinterfragt. 1922 schuf Outerbridge eine der Ikonen dieser photographischen Wesensforschung, ›*Ide Collar*‹ (Taf. 9), als Auftrag für eine Produktaufnahme. Die Photographie zeigt in schräger Aufsicht einen damals noch gebräuchlichen Einsatzkragen, der in offener, elliptischer Form über einem asymmetrisch verschobenen Schachbrett zu schweben scheint. Die Simplizität in der Dinghaftigkeit der dargestellten Gegenstände, desgleichen der in der Komposition erreichte Abstraktionsgrad begeisterten Duchamp bei der Entdeckung der Anzeige in *Vanity Fair* derart, daß er ein geistesverwandtes Readymade in ihr erkannte und sie an die Wand seines Studios heftete. Nachdem sich Outerbridge in seiner Arbeit für mondäne Modemagazine eine Reputation als stilsicherer und werbewirksamer Photograph und Graphikdesigner erworben hatte, begann 1925 in Paris für ihn eine Periode des Expatriotismus. Die Erfolge in der Heimat und Outerbridges weltläufiger Charme öffneten ihm die Pforten zu Künstlerateliers, Agenturen und zur Condé Nast-Redaktion, als deren Layouter für das Modemagazin *Vogue* er tätig wurde. Zu seinen Kollegen gehörte ein anderer Erneuerer amerikanischer Photokunst, der spätere Leiter der photographischen Abteilung am Museum of Modern Art in New York, Edward Steichen. Als Outerbridge kündigte, um eine freiberufliche Laufbahn zu verfolgen, entstand zwischen beiden ein amüsanter Wettkampf, in dem das Ei in 4000 Variationen die 1000 Teetassen Steichens übertrumpfte. Die Ironie wollte es, daß Steichen wie Outerbridge gleichermaßen abstrahierende, doch in konzeptueller Anlage grundverschiedene Versionen mit dem Titel ›*The Triumph of the Egg*‹ (Taf. 11) vorlegten. Die Eröffnung von Outerbridges Pariser Photoatelier, für das er keine Kosten (und vermutlich keinen Aufwand an Publicity) in der Installation modernster Atelier- und Lichttechnik scheute, wurde in der Fachwelt als furioses Ereignis gefeiert. Auch die Spötter waren nicht weit, als der große Augenblick gekommen war und der Meister zum Auftakt seine erste Aufnahme schaffen sollte, der zwischen künstlerischer Konzeption und ihrer Durchführung keine technischen Hürden mehr im Wege stehen würden. Nach Monaten gespannten Wartens wurde das Kunstwerk geboren, und es war – das Photo eines Eies! Das ehrgeizige Atelier erwies sich schnell als finanzielles Fiasko und mußte aufgegeben werden. Nach einem filmischen Intermezzo in Berlin und London, in dem er für die deutschen Regisseure Georg Wilhelm Pabst und E. A. Dupont als kameratechnischer Berater wirkte, kehrte Outerbridge 1929 nach New York zurück.

search for essence, *"Ide Collar"* (Plate 9), as a commission for a product photograph. In a slanting view from above, the photograph shows an example of the type of detachable collar then in use, which seems to be floating in an open, elliptical shape over an asymmetrically placed chessboard. When Duchamp came across the advert in *Vanity Fair* and saw the simplicity and materiality of the objects presented, and also the degree of abstraction achieved in the composition, he was so enthusiastic that he immediately saw it as a "readymade" by a kindred spirit, and pinned it to his studio wall.

In 1925, after Outerbridge had made his reputation as a stylistically confident and effective advertising photographer and graphic designer through his work for chic fashion magazines, he began a period as an expatriate in Paris. His success at home, as well as his own cosmopolitan charm, gave him access to artists' studios, agencies, and the Condé Nast editorial offices, where he was hired as layout designer for the fashion magazine *Vogue*. One of his colleagues there was another innovator in American photography and later director of the photographic department at the Museum of Modern Art in New York, Edward Steichen. When Outerbridge resigned from *Vogue* in order to pursue a freelance career, an amusing rivalry arose between the two, in which Outerbridge's egg in 4000 variations finally won out over Steichen's 1000 teacups. Ironically, both Steichen and Outerbridge produced equally abstract, but in their conceptual approach fundamentally different, photographs under the title *The Triumph of the Egg* (Plate 11). Outerbridge spared no expense (and probably no publicity costs) in equipping and installing his new Paris studio with the most modern studio and lighting technology, and its opening was looked forward to by photographic experts as a wildly important event. The mockers were not far off, however, when the great moment at last came. The master was to take his first photograph in the new studio to mark the opening, a photograph for which there would at last be no more technical obstacles remaining between the artistic concept and its realization. After months of tense expectation the work of art was born, and it was – a photo of an egg! The ambitious studio soon proved to be a financial fiasco and had to be abandoned. After an interval involved in films in Berlin and London, during which he worked as an adviser on camera technique for the German director Georg Wilhelm Pabst and for E.A. Dupont, Paul Outerbridge returned to New York in 1929.

Black-and-white photography held no more secrets for him, and he decided instead "to make the best color photographs that have ever been made anywhere by anyone."[3] The carbro-color process offered the ideal conditions for per-

Die Schwarzweiß-Photographie barg für ihn zu jenem Zeitpunkt keine Geheimnisse mehr, und er beschloß, »die besten Farbaufnahmen zu machen, die jemals von irgend jemandem irgendwo gemacht worden sind«.[3] Das Carbro-Color-Verfahren bot die idealen Voraussetzungen zur Perfektionierung von Material und Technik. »Trotz meiner beachtlichen Erfahrung auf dem Gebiet der Photographie war ich eine ganze Zeit lang nicht sicher, ob es mir jemals gelingen würde, einen guten Carbro-Abzug herzustellen. Viele dieser Bilder entstanden unter erheblichen technischen Schwierigkeiten, die den heutigen Benutzern der neueren und wesentlich einfacheren Farbmaterialien unbekannt sind. Jede Einstellung kostete 150 Dollar, und man brauchte viele Arbeitsstunden, um sie herzustellen. Drei verschiedene Aufnahmen mit unterschiedlichen Belichtungszeiten mußten mit drei verschiedenen Farbfiltern gemacht werden. Dann mußten drei separate Farbbilder, nur 1/10.000stel Inch stark, paßgenau eins über das andere auf das Papier übertragen werden.«[4] Waren schon seine Schwarzweiß-Vergrößerungen wertvolle Sammlerstükke, von denen er nur wenige Exemplare zog, um anschließend das Negativ zu zerstören, erklomm der manische Perfektionist Outerbridge in der Entwicklung seiner Farbästhetik neue Höhepunkte, um die »absolute Gewißheit« der Farbe zu erzielen. »Die falsche Wiedergabe von Farben in Schwarzweiß bringt oft faszinierende tonale Kontraste und dynamische Bilder hervor, aber bei der Farbphotographie ist das anders, die geringste Abweichung der Farben fällt deutlich ins Auge und ist völlig unannehmbar.«[5] Die dreißiger Jahre widmete er dem intensiven Studium und der Verfeinerung seiner Farbtechnik, doch den Zenit zweier inspirierter, schöpferischer Dekaden schien er mit der Übersiedlung nach Kalifornien, 1943, überschritten zu haben. Bis zu seinem Tod 1958 arbeitete er für Einrichtungs- und Wohnmagazine, publizierte Bücher und Kolumnen über die Photographie und verwaltete die Mode- und Designfirma seiner zweiten Frau.

Der olfaktorische Akt

In jahrhundertelanger Zivilisationsarbeit ist der Geruchssinn immer mehr als ein niederer ausgegrenzt worden. Obwohl er unser erster Vermittler von Eindrücken der nächsten Umgebung ist, wird er selten aktiviert in der Rezeption der bildenden Künste, der gigantischen Flut von Printmedien oder gar der gegenwärtigen elektronischen Unterhaltungsindustrie. Im Erfahren der mechanischen Reproduzierbarkeit von sterilen Gegenstands- und Bildwelten wird der bereits von Kant als der edelste postulierte Gesichtssinn zum ausschließlichen

fecting the materials and technique. "Despite my considerable experience in the field of photography, I was for a long time unsure whether I would ever succeed in producing a good carbro print. Many of these pictures were produced with considerable technical difficulties unknown to today's users of more recent and much simpler color materials. Each shot cost $150, and many hours of work were necessary to produce it. Three different shots with varying exposures had to be made with three different color filters. After this, three separate color images each one thousandth of an inch thick had to be transferred onto the paper one by one and precisely superimposed one on top of the other."[4] While his black-and-white enlargements had already been collector's items for which he only made a few prints before destroying the negative, the fanatical perfectionist scaled new heights in developing his color aesthetics, aiming to achieve "absolute certainty" in color. "The false reproduction of color using black and white often produces fascinating tonal contrasts and dynamic images, but in color photography it is different, as the least deviation in the colors is immediately noticeable and entirely unacceptable."[5] During the 1930s, Outerbridge devoted himself to studying and refining his color technique, but when he moved to California in 1943, he seemed to have passed the peak of his two inspired, creative decades. Until his death in 1958 he worked for interior decoration and design magazines, published books and wrote magazine columns on photography, and ran his second wife's fashion and design business.

The Olfactory Nude

During the centuries-long process of the growth of civilization, the sense of smell has more and more been excluded as something base and primitive. Although it is the primary mediator of sense impressions from our immediate vicinity, it is rarely activated during the reception of impressions from the fine arts, the gigantic flood of printed media, or even in the contemporary electronic entertainment industry. Now that the mechanical reproduction of sterile worlds of objects and images has become possible, the sense of sight, considered by Kant to be the noblest, has become the exclusive transmitter of perceptions from an environment in which visual stimuli are rampant. At the beginning of the 1930s, Outerbridge stood on the verge of the era of color reproduction – in which familiar images today range from micro-organisms to the whole of the blue planet Earth – and he was working with relatively primitive techniques of color processing. He de-

Transmittor zwischen unserer Wahrnehmung und einer an visuellen Reizen überbordenden Umwelt. An der Schwelle zur farbigen Wiedergabe von Mikro-Organismen bis hin zum blauen Planeten Erde mit noch relativ unausgereiften Techniken in Kolorverfahren, verläßt Outerbridge zu Beginn der dreißiger Jahre das für ihn langweilig gewordene Terrain der Schwarzweiß-Photographie, um sich den Herausforderungen der Farbphotographie zu stellen. Mit dem Spektrum der Grautonskala in der Schwarzweiß-Photographie verbindet sich jedoch bis zum heutigen Tage ein artifizielles, verfremdendes Moment, da wir die Welt nun einmal farbig sehen und erleben. Für das Genre der Aktphotographie bedeutet dies, daß sie der Abbildung des menschlichen Körpers den unmittelbaren Schrecken nimmt, die zivilisatorische Scham vor nackter Haut, da sie diese mit einem gnädigen Grauschleier kaschiert. Dem in puritanischen Grundfesten verankerten amerikanischen Publikum präsentierten sich Outerbridges Akte in ihrer brillanten Farbwiedergabe in einer bis dahin nie gesehenen, drastischen Realitätsnähe. Für eine asketischen Idealen huldigende Gesellschaft war dies ein Schock, ein Skandal, der den erfolgreichen Photographen Outerbridge ins kommerzielle Abseits manövrierte und schließlich das Ende seiner photographischen Karriere bedeutete.

Der Körper, den Paul Valéry »das einzigartige, das wahre, das ewige, das vollständige, das unübersteigbare *Referenzsystem*«[6] nannte, war für John Doe, den amerikanischen Durchschnittsbürger nach der Prohibition (auch diese eine Erfindung bigotter Frauenvereine zur Unterbindung von Sinnlichkeit), die *terra incognita* schlechthin. Und nun kamen Outerbridges Frauen: Aktaufnahmen in Farben und von einer haptischen Qualität, die die Haut der Modelle geradezu fühlbar machten; delikate Aderverzweigungen unter alabasternem Schimmer können vom Auge ertastet werden; rasierte Venushügel und Schamzonen ohne jede Retouche; delikate rosige Mulden und Faltungen – der Duft der Frauen strömt aus diesen Photographien, ein Affront für das schlichte Gemüt eines jeden guten Amerikaners. Jedoch für den Seher, der sich auf die Wanderschaft begibt, das »Abenteuer Epidermis«, das neben dem Gesichtssinn auch andere Sinne kitzelt.

Vom Dandy zum *Playboy*

»Das Leben ist für jedermann der Akt seines Körpers«[7], so noch einmal Valéry. Des Wortes doppelte Bedeutung wird in den Akten von Paul Outerbridge evident. Der Photograph, der sich in seiner Schwarzweiß-Periode während der *Golden Twenties* in einem berühmten Selbstportrait (Taf. 6) noch mit den

cided to abandon the realm of black- and-white photography, which he had come to find tedious, and move forward to face the challenges of color photography. The spectrum of the gray scale associated with black-and- white photography even today, however, is associated with an element of artificiality and alienation, since it is simply an unavoidable fact that we do see and experience the world in color. In the genre of nude photography, this meant that the depiction of the human body lost its initial shock, civilization's embarrassment over naked skin, as it was mercifully concealed behind a gray veil. Outerbridge's nudes, in brilliant color reproduction and with a drastic, hitherto unparalleled realism, were seen by an American public firmly anchored in its Puritan foundations. For a society that valued ascetic ideals, it was a shock, and it caused a scandal that pushed Outerbridge, till then a successful photographer, into the commercial wilderness and ultimately meant the end of his career as a photographer.

The body, referred to by Paul Valéry as "the unique, the true, the eternal, the perfect, the insurmountable *reference system*"[6] was simply *terra incognita* to John Doe, the average American citizen at the end of Prohibition (which also had its origins in efforts by bigoted women's associations to repress sensuality). And now came Outerbridge's women: nude photographs in color that have a haptic quality that makes the models' skin almost touchable; the eye can feel its way along delicate arterial branches under an alabaster sheen; shaved montes veneris and pudenda without the slightest retouching; delicate, pink hollows and folds – the scent of women streams from the photographs, affronting the plain soul of every good American. But for an observer prepared to go "wandering," it was an "adventure of the epidermis," exciting senses other than that of sight.

From Dandy to Playboy

"For everyone, life is an act of the body,"[7] as Valéry also wrote. During Outerbridge's black-and-white period in the "Golden Twenties," he produced a famous self-portrait (Plate 6) in which he is dressed up in all the insignia of a dandy, at the same time distorting these symbols to make them grotesque – the top hat worn above a mask resembling racing driver's or diver's goggles, with an Adolphe Menjou mustache, stand-up collar, a dickey inside his tuxedo and the obligatory (canary yellow?) Baudelairean glove. Outerbridge left all the traditional views of the nude behind. From the powdered, shimmering boudoirs of the bohemian world the dandy entered the cool, satin glitter of Art Déco salons, building

Insignien des Dandys schmückt, um sie gleichzeitig ins Groteske zu verzerren – der *Chapeau claque* über einer Maske – halb Rennfahrer-, halb Taucherbrille, Adolphe Menjou-Bärtchen, Vatermörder, Wespeneinsatz im Smoking und der obligate (kanariengelbe?) Baudelaire'sche Handschuh –, läßt die traditionelle Auffassung vom Akt hinter sich. Aus den reispudrig flimmernden Boudoirs der Bohème tritt der Dandy in den satinkühlen Glanz der Art déco-Salons, die er selbst in seinem Atelier in Nyack, Upstate New York, konstruiert. Dort beginnt er einen spielerischen Diskurs mit dem von ihm favorisierten Modell – der Frau. Die übliche Rollenverteilung zwischen Photographierendem und seinem Objekt (der Begierde) wird obsolet. Unklar ist, wer mit wem spielt. Oder aber der Photograph wird von seinem Modell, das sich wie Danae in einer Art lasziver Selbstvergessenheit rekelt (*Reclining Nude,* Liegender Akt, Taf. 43), ganz einfach ignoriert. Ob sie sich an Säulen oder Wände schmiegt, wohlgefällig ihr Spiegelbild betrachtet – wobei das männliche Idol Clark Gable, hinter den Spiegel gesteckt, zur Bedeutungslosigkeit schrumpft (*Nude sitting at dressing table,* Sitzender Akt am Frisiertisch, Taf. 33) –, ob sie sich selbst berührt oder in einen Dialog mit dem Betrachter/Photographen tritt – stets des eigenen Körpers, ihrer Schönheit bewußt –, benutzen lassen sich die Frauen auf Outerbridges Akten nicht. Eine solche Balance, die gerade in diesem Genre so oft zum Nachteil des weiblichen Geschlechts in eine pornographische Okkupierbarkeit und Kommerzialisierung umkippt, die dem menschlichen Körper einen Warencharakter aufprägt, scheint hier noch ungefährdet. Mittels eines unbedingten Gestaltungswillens und eines offensichtlichen ästhetischen Vergnügens auf seiten des Photographen und im Akt des ebenso genußvollen Erlebens ihrer Körper auf seiten der Modelle wird dem Betrachter nicht nur der »Akt des Aktes«, sondern ein ungewöhnliches Equilibrium harmonischen Einverständnisses vorgeführt. Ein ähnlich stimmiger Gleichklang zwischen Modell und Photograph herrscht auf den *Storyville Portraits* von E. J. Bellocq, auf denen Prostituierte in New Orleans vergleichbar gelassen und selbstbewußt in die Kamera blicken.

Diese Positionierung des »Wer spiegelt sich in wem?« ist als klassisch-psychologisches Motiv des Narziß natürlich auch in Outerbridges Akten angelegt; von größerer Bedeutung mag jedoch das Moment des Fetischismus für die Interpretation seiner Arbeiten sein. Wir werden später auf diesen Aspekt zurückkommen. Für Outerbridge liegt das Interesse an der Abbildung des menschlichen Körpers in einer Form des Narziß-Komplexes begründet, die der gesamten Menschheit zu eigen ist. Julia Kristeva bestätigt dem mythischen Narziß eine größere Affinität zum modernen Menschen: »Er bricht

one himself in his studio in Nyack in upstate New York. It was here that he began his dialogue with the model he preferred – the female. The usual division of roles between the one taking photographs and the object (of desire) becomes obsolete. It is not clear who is playing with whom here. Or perhaps the photographer is simply being ignored by his model, who is stretching like Danaë in a kind of lascivious absent-mindedness (*Reclining Nude,* Plate 43). Whether she is leaning against pillars or walls, looking contentedly at her image in the mirror while the male idol Clark Gable, hidden behind the mirror, shrinks to insignificance (*Nude Sitting at Dressing Table,* Plate 33), whether she touches herself or enters into dialogue with the observer/photographer, always conscious of her own body, her own beauty – the women in Outerbridge's nudes never allow themselves to be used. This balance, which especially in this genre often tips over to women's disadvantage into a pornographic commercialization that stamps the human body with the quality of a commodity, seems not yet to be threatened here. With an absolute will to achieve structure and an obvious aesthetic pleasure on the photographer's part, and on the part of the model an equally pleasurable experience of her own body, the observer is shown not merely a "nude," but an extraordinary equilibrium of harmonious understanding. A comparable harmony between the model and the photographer is seen in E. J. Bellocq's *Storyville Portraits,* in which New Orleans prostitutes gaze into the camera in a similarly relaxed and self-aware way.

This establishment of a "who is being mirrored by whom?" problem is of course present as a classically psychological Narcissus motif in Outerbridge's nudes as well. But of greater significance for the interpretation of his work is the element of fetishism in it, a point we will return to below. For Outerbridge, the interest in creating an image of the human body lies in a form of the Narcissus complex, which is common to all of humanity. Julia Kristeva asserts that the mythical Narcissus has a tremendous affinity for modern humanity: "He breaks with the antique world because he makes himself the origin of seeing, and seeks the other facing him as the product of his own seeing. In this he discovers that this image is not another, but that he himself has presented it, that the other is a self-representation. In this way, and in a manner opposed to that of mysticism, Narcissus discovers in pain and in death the constitutive alienation of his own image."[8]

A new self-awareness among women in the USA during the 1930s grew out of their increasing acceptance in the working world. Their growing share in the economic life of

mit der antiken Welt, weil er sich zum Ursprung des Schauens macht und den anderen ihm gegenüber als Produkt seines Schauens sucht. Er entdeckt dabei, daß dieses Abbild nicht ein anderer ist, sondern daß er ihn selbst vorstellt, daß der andere die Selbstvorstellung ist. Auf diese Weise also, und durch einen der Mystik entgegengesetzten Weg, entdeckt Narziß im Schmerz und im Tod die konstitutive Entfremdung des eigenen Bildes.«[8]

Ein neues Selbstverständnis der Frauen war in den USA der dreißiger Jahre Ausdruck eines durch größere berufliche Akzeptanz veränderten Bewußtseins. Ihr vermehrter wirtschaftsbedingter Einsatz im krisengeschüttelten Amerika des New Deal förderte auch ihre Emanzipation. Den exzellenten, selbstironischen Eskapaden solcher Entertainerinnen wie Mae West und Jean Harlow schob das reaktionäre und zensurgeile Hays Office jedoch rasch den Riegel vor das unverhohlen erotische und bitterböse Mundwerk. Zu stark durften diese »Weibsbilder« nicht werden. Die Parade der Hollywood-Diven wurde geschliffen, von der sexuellen Schärfe blieb mitunter ein sarkastischer Biß, und der »battle of sexes« wurde nach 1933 zu einem partnerschaftlichen Gerangel befriedet. Allerdings sucht der Schlagabtausch der gemischtgeschlechtlichen Screwballs der nun folgenden Komödien an rhetorischer Brillanz bis heute seinesgleichen. Was Hollywood dem prüden Amerika laut offizieller Verordnung subtiler verpacken mußte, wurde in den Kinosälen weitergeträumt und in Outerbridges Studio an der Ostküste des Landes in Fleisch und Blut extrapoliert.

Eine gewisse »cleane« oder auch kosmetische Anmutung seiner Aufnahmen ist zum einen der Farbphotographie immanent; zum anderen entspricht sie einer in den USA zwischen den Kriegen vorherrschenden Ästhetik. Diese ist, stets verkaufsstrategisch orientiert, oft eine enge Symbiose mit der Werbung eingegangen. Den gesellschaftlich aufoktroyierten Restriktionen gemäß, war der nackte Körper eigentlich verpönt; die kapitalistische Grundeinstellung und im Zuge aufweichender Moral stetig permissiver werdende Verhaltensmuster in der sozialen Interaktion ließen jedoch immer mehr Haut in Reklamebilder eindringen. In Vargas' stromlinienförmigen, nahezu geschlechtslosen Pin-ups findet dieses ästhetische Ideal am Beispiel der Frau seine ultimative Ausformung.

In derselben Zeitspanne arbeiten sich Photographen wie Josef Sudek oder André Kertész an den abstrakten, surrealen Distorsionen ihrer Akte ab, versieht Man Ray seine solarisierten Modelle mit einer ätherischen zweiten »Photohaut«, schafft schwerelose Torsi, die nicht von dieser Welt sein können. Doch alle bleiben sie jener Tradition der Aktphotogra-

crisis-ridden New Deal America also encouraged their emancipation. Entertainers such as Mae West and Jean Harlow, however, with their superb, self-ironic escapades, soon had their openly erotic and even vicious statements clamped down on by the reactionary censorship of the Hays Office. The "wenches" were not to get above themselves. A parade of Hollywood divas was manufactured, and although a certain sarcastic touch could still occasionally be noted as a leftover from the earlier sexual toughness, after 1933 the "battle of the sexes" was reduced to squabbles between couples. Nevertheless, the verbal exchanges between the mixed-sex screwballs in the later comedies have never been matched in their rhetorical brilliance. What Hollywood, under official instructions, had to wrap up more subtly for prudish America continued to be dreamt about in the movie theaters; and in Outerbridge's studio on the east coast it was extrapolated into flesh and blood.

A certain "clean" or cosmetic appearance in his photographs is, on the one hand, inevitable in color photography; on the other hand, it corresponds to an aesthetics that was dominant in the USA between the wars. It is an aesthetics which, always oriented towards sales strategies, was symbiotically absorbed into advertising. In accordance with socially imposed restrictions, the naked body was frowned on; but basic capitalist attitudes and – with relaxing moral standards – ever more permissive behavior patterns in social interactions led to more and more skin appearing in advertising images. In Vargas's streamlined, almost sexless pin-ups, this aesthetic ideal reached its ultimate refinement in relation to the female body.

In the same period, photographers such as Josef Sudek or André Kertész were working on abstract, surreal distortions of their nudes, and Man Ray decorated his solarized models with an ethereal second "photoskin" and produced weightless torsos that seem to be from another world. But all of them remained bound to a tradition of nude photography that attempts to elevate the body, to transcend it, to deprive it of its nudity. It would have been unthinkable for these representatives of a black-and-white ideology to suddenly start working in color. For his time, Outerbridge was too advanced to be able to find broad public acceptance for his nude studies; his presentation of the flesh was too vivid and, like nineteenth-century erotic images, was suspected of being indecent. He produced his work for a small group of potential clients who even then were prepared to pay four-figure sums for the valuable prints.

Despite all the moral indignation and lack of understanding for Outerbridge's art during the 1930s, his brilliant real-

phie verhaftet, die versucht, den Körper zu erhöhen, ihn zu transzendieren, ihm »das Nackte« zu rauben. Undenkbar für jene Repräsentanten einer Schwarzweiß-Ideologie, nun plötzlich in Farbe zu operieren. Outerbridge war für seine Zeit zu modern, um für die realistischen Oberflächen seiner Aktaufnahmen eine breite Zustimmung im Publikum zu finden; die Darstellung des Fleisches war zu lebendig und kam, wie bei erotischen Darstellungen des 19. Jahrhunderts, in den Ruf, unanständig zu sein. Er produzierte für eine kleine Gruppe von potenten Käufern, die schon damals bereit waren, die wertvollen Prints mit vierstelligen Summen zu honorieren.

Aller moralischen Entrüstung und allem Unverständnis für Outerbridges Kunst in den dreißiger Jahren zum Trotz ebnete sein brillanter Realismus in ironischer Umkehr den Weg zur populistischen und trivial-vulgären Vermarktung des weiblichen Körpers: Eine Gesellschaft wird von ihren eigenen Schlüpfrigkeiten eingeholt. 1953, kaum fünfzehn Jahre nach den ersten farbigen Akten, sollte Hugh Hefner in der restaurativen Jahrhundertmitte mit seinem Konzept der ewig verfügbaren, sich widerstandslos anbietenden Eva, hochglanzpoliert und faltenlos aseptisch, den Siegeszug bei frustrierten Ehemännern rund um den Globus antreten. Wo bei Outerbridge eigenwillige Modelle aktiv an der Produktion von Phantasien (der eigenen oder fremder) mitwirkten, degradierte der *Playboy* die Frau zur passiven Sexmieze. Der witzigen und fordernden Aggressivität der Screwballs und den körperbewußten Frauen bei Outerbridge wurde in der auf traditionelle Werte fixierten Eisenhower-Dekade vollends der Garaus gemacht: Phantasien von Männern für Männer unter Ausschließung der weiblichen Imago, Entfremdung der Frau von ihrem eigenen Begehren. Mr. Hefner bediente die konditionierte männliche Wahrnehmung in möglichst plakativer Form unter der Maxime der amerikanischen Verkaufsflagge – »easy to consume«. Outerbridges Leerstellen, Orte, an denen sich durch eine spielerische Symbolik und mittels fetischistischer Versatzstücke die Vorstellungskraft des Betrachters ausagieren konnte, wurden durch eine banale *Playboy*-Ästhetik plattgewalzt. Der amerikanische Kulturkritiker Clement Greenberg veröffentlichte bereits 1939 seine präzise Definition jener »Ersatzkultur« und des Kitsches, die sich erst nach dem Zweiten Weltkrieg und auf neu etablierten Absatzmärkten bei einer nach farbigen Printmedien hungrigen Konsumgesellschaft voll entfalten konnten. Television war noch eine seltene Kommodität. »Kitsch, der als Rohmaterial die entwurzelten und akademischen Simulakren einer echten Kultur verwendet, begrüßt und kultiviert diese Unsensibilität. Dies ist die Quelle seiner Profite. Kitsch ist mechanisch und arbeitet mit Formeln. Kitsch bedeutet nachempfundene Erfahrung und

ism ironically opened the way for the populist, trivial, and vulgar marketing of the female body: society was overtaken by its own lewdness. In 1953, little more than fifteen years after the first color nudes and during the mid-century period of restoration, Hugh Hefner was to start his victory march among frustrated husbands all over the world with his idea for an ever-available, unresisting Eve, shining and wrinkle-free. Where models with minds of their own took an active share in the production of fantasies (their own or others') in Outerbridge's work, *Playboy* degraded women into passive sex kittens. The witty, challenging aggressiveness of the screwballs and of Outerbridge's women, aware of their own bodies, was completely extinguished in the Eisenhower decade, which was fixated on traditional values: what remained were fantasies produced by men for men that excluded the female imago and alienated women from their own desires. Hefner exploited conditioned male perceptions to the utmost, using the slogan of American sales strategy – "easy to consume." The blank spaces left by Outerbridge, places in which playful symbolism and fetishistic settings can release the observer's imagination, were steamrollered by the banal *Playboy* aesthetics. As early as 1939, the American critic Clement Greenberg published his precise definition of the "substitute culture" and kitsch that only reached its full development after the Second World War and in newly established markets in a consumer society hungry for new print media. Television was still a rare commodity. "Kitsch, using for raw material the debased and academicized simulacra of genuine culture, welcomes and cultivates this insensibility. It is the source of its profits. Kitsch is mechanical and operates by formulas. Kitsch is vicarious experience and faked sensa-tions. Kitsch changes according to style, but remains always the same. Kitsch is the epitome of all that is spurious in the life of our times. Kitsch pretends to demand nothing of its customers except their money – not even their time."[9]

Path between Seduction and Eroticism

"I met a girl who devoted herself totally to her lover, only she refused to take off her hat because it suited her so well."[10] Francis Picabia, Funny Guy Dada, would certainly have a lot to say on this topic, but this introductory aphorism must suffice. Outerbridge's mask and top hat from the self-portrait mentioned above, or rubber bathing caps, are used by the women in a series of color nudes as disguises, as scanty costumes, as challenges, or as paths of retreat from erotic

gefälschte Sinneseindrücke. Kitsch verändert sich, was Stil anbelangt, bleibt sich jedoch selbst stets treu. Kitsch ist der Inbegriff all dessen, was in unseren Zeiten unecht ist. Kitsch gibt vor, den Konsumenten nichts außer ihrem Geld abzuverlangen – noch nicht einmal ihre Zeit.«[9]

Pfade zwischen Verführung und Erotik

»Ich habe ein junges Mädchen kennengelernt, das sich ihrem Geliebten ganz hingab, nur wollte sie ihren Hut nicht abnehmen unter dem Vorwand, er stünde ihr so gut.«[10] Funny Guy Dada, Francis Picabia, könnte sicher vieles zum Thema beitragen. Belassen wir es bei diesem einleitenden Aphorismus. Maske und Zylinder aus Outerbridges oben beschriebenem Selbstportrait oder Badekappen aus Gummi dienen den Frauen in einer Reihe von farbigen Akten zur Verkleidung, zum »dürftigen« Kostüm, zur Herausforderung oder zum Rückzug im erotischen Flirt. Ob die Vorliebe Outerbridges für Masken und derlei Tand rein spielerischer Natur ist oder Fetischcharakter trägt, bleibt der Spekulation anheimgestellt. Selbst der Vater der Psychoanalyse weiß in seiner Abhandlung über den Fetischismus keinen genauen Rat: »Der Kastrationsschreck beim Anblick des weiblichen Genitales bleibt wahrscheinlich keinem männlichen Wesen erspart. Warum die einen infolge dieses Eindruckes homosexuell werden, die anderen ihn durch die Schöpfung eines Fetischs abwehren und die übergroße Mehrzahl ihn überwindet, das wissen wir freilich nicht zu erklären.«[11] Die Maske als Feigenblatt, das primäre Geschlechtsmerkmale preisgibt, dafür das Irritierendste oder Bedrohlichste im erotischen Diskurs verbirgt: den Blick des Gegenübers. Der Photograph treibt Fairplay mit seinen Modellen. Wenn, dann sind alle Beteiligten am Spiel Voyeure oder keine. Die ihn nur als Kamera-Auge wahrnehmen, dürfen auch sich selbst manchmal verstecken. Die Szenarien, die hier präsentiert werden, wecken Assoziationen an Dressurakte im Zirkuszelt: Outerbridge als Dompteur weiblicher und eigener Paarungsinstinkte und erotischen Begehrens. Die eigenen sexuellen Begierden werden im Akt des Photographierens/der Dressur gezügelt und sublimiert.

Eine weitere Variante: Die Modelle in der Umkehrung des Verhältnisses »La belle et la bête« erzeugen neue Dichotomien. Frauen als »wilde Tiere« in mehrdeutiger Ergebungsgeste mit erhobenen Armen, postiert an der Wand des Studio-Käfigs, doch vibrierend vor elegant-gezähmter Energie, die jederzeit auszubrechen vermag. Nicht das buchstäbliche mit-dem-Rücken-an-der-Wand-Stehen des in die Enge Getriebenen wird zelebriert, nein, das Selbstbewußtsein ist so

flirting. It remains a matter of speculation whether Outerbridge's taste for masks and trinkets was purely playful, or whether it was fetishistic in quality. Even Freud was uncertain in his discussion of fetishism: "The fear of castration when looking at the female genitals is probably shared by all males. Why it should be that some of them become homosexual as a result of this impression, while others resist it by creating a fetish, and the vast majority overcome it, we admittedly cannot at the moment explain."[11] The mask serves as a fig leaf revealing the primary sexual characteristics, but concealing the most irritating or threatening element in erotic discourse: the partner's glance. The photographer is fair to his models. Either everyone in the game is a voyeur or no one. Those who perceive him only as the eye of the camera are sometimes allowed to conceal themselves as well. The scenarios presented here have connotations of animal taming in the circus tent: Outerbridge is the tamer both of female mating instincts and of his own, the tamer of erotic desire. His own sexual desires are restrained and sublimated in the act of photography/taming.

Or another variation: the models, reversing the relationship of "Beauty and the Beast," produce new dichotomies. Women as "wild animals" in ambiguous gestures of surrender with raised arms, posed against the wall of the studio cage, but vibrating with elegantly tamed energy that could break out at any time. What is being celebrated here is not the literal standing with one's back to the wall of those who have been cornered; no, their self-confidence is so limitless that they turn their bare backs to the observer. Then again there are the claws from Balinese dance, pressed into the model's own flesh, but ready for the attack (*Woman with Claws,* Plate 22). The flickering in these women's eyes is unbearable, and the eyes have to be concealed behind masks to ease the tension in the duel of glances. Who is taming who here? "...Seduction does not stop in the truth of signs, but in deception and secrecy; it reveals a mode of circulation which is itself ritual and secret, a kind of immediate initiation that follows only its own rules."[12] In the polarity between calculating strategy and sensuous animality in the menagerie of seduction, woman has long since stripped the tamer of his uniform (*Nude with Bandleader's Jacket,* Plate 37) and exposed him helplessly to her self-sufficient, narcissistic magic. Even Apollo, god of poetry and measure in Greek mythology, passes away into the iron-soft embrace of female nakedness (*"Phoenix Rising",* Plate 24). In an ironic reversal of roles, sexes, and millenia-old idolatries, the Apollonian tectonics of the composition literally inscribe the woman's pudenda on the beautiful young man's head.

grenzenlos, daß sie dem Betrachter den blanken Rücken zuwenden. Oder die balinesischen Tanzkrallen, noch ins eigene Fleisch gepreßt, doch bereit zum Angriff (*Woman with claws,* Frau mit Klauen, Taf. 22). Unerträglich das Flackern in den Augen dieser Frauen, die durch Masken camoufliert werden müssen, um dem Kräftemessen im Duell der Blicke die Schärfe zu nehmen.

Wer bezwingt hier wen? » ... die Verführung macht niemals bei der Wahrheit der Zeichen halt, sondern bei der Täuschung und beim Geheimnis, sie eröffnet einen Zirkulationsmodus, der selbst geheim und rituell ist, eine Art unmittelbarer Initiation, die nur ihrer eigenen Spielregel folgt.«[12] (Baudrillard) In der Polarität zwischen kalkulierter Strategie und sinnlicher Animalität in der Menagerie der Verführung hat die Frau dem Dompteur längst seine Uniform abgezwungen (*Nude with bandleader's jacket,* Akt mit Jacke des Bandleaders, Taf. 37) und setzt ihn hilflos ihrem selbstgenügsamen, narzißtischen Zauber aus. Sogar Apollon, Gott der Dichtkunst und des Maßes in der griechischen Mythologie, vergeht in der eisenweichen Umschlingung weiblicher Nacktheit (›*Phoenix Rising*‹, Taf. 24). In ironischer Verkehrung von Rollen, Geschlechtern und jahrtausendealten Idolatrien wird in der apollinischen Tektonik dieser Komposition dem schönen Jüngling buchstäblich die Scham der Frau an den Kopf gedichtet.

Erotik erzeugt oder stimuliert Begehren, ein Begehren, das sich nicht nur in dem Anderen entfacht, sondern zuerst in dem Selbst. Es ist also von reflexiver Qualität. Anwürfen, in den Werken Outerbridges oder jenen seiner Adepten wie Helmut Newton recke die Pornographie ihr häßlich Haupt, sei hier jeglicher Zündstoff genommen. Wiewohl Newton im Exhibitionismus und Voyeurismus seiner »participants du jeu« entschieden weiter geht. In einem ausgewogenen Diskurs unter Teilnehmern, die sich ihrer Markierungen im Diagramm der Kräfte bewußt sind, kann es kein Moment der Ausbeutung geben. – Nur die vakanten Positionen, die von der Phantasie der Spieler und Betrachter besetzt werden können.

Über die Schönheit der Frauen

Schon Man Ray behauptete, einen Akt zu photographieren sei die schwierigste Aufgabe überhaupt, und je schöner das Modell, desto schwieriger sei es, etwas zu schaffen, was ihm gerecht werde. Nun hat sich Outerbridge nicht nur praktisch diesem Problem genähert, sondern auch in mehreren theoretischen Abhandlungen die Frage nach der weiblichen Schönheit gestellt und wie sie photographisch zu fixieren sei. In einem Traktat aus dem Jahre 1933 proklamiert er die Treue

The erotic produces or stimulates desire, a desire aroused not only by others, but also by oneself. It thus has a reflexive quality. Accusations that pornography is raising its ugly head in Outerbridge's work, or in the work of his disciples such as Helmut Newton, can be easily disarmed, although Newton goes a decisive step further in the exhibitionism and voyeurism of his *participants du jeu.* In a balanced discourse among participants who are conscious of their places in the geometry of energies, there can be no element of exploitation; only vacant positions that can be occupied by the fantasies of the players and observers.

Feminine Beauty

Even Man Ray said that photographing a nude was the most difficult thing possible, and the more beautiful the model, the more difficult it was to produce a photograph that would do her justice. Outerbridge not only approached this problem in practice, but also explored the nature of feminine beauty and how to record it photographically in several theoretical essays. In a text written in 1933, he proclaimed that one should be true to one's own sex, and appealed to a femininity that modern women had lost. Basing his view on the classical ideal of the *Venus de Milo,* he described ingeniously, and with the eye of a connoisseur, the relationships between the proportions of the female body, and emphasized as the main characteristics of this harmonious structure its softness and its curves. As an example of the twenty-eight points of his examination, corresponding, according to Outerbridge, to the 28 days of the lunar cycle, we may take his description of the trunk or torso, "which in a beautiful body should be full and round, deep-chested – above all, *not* like many American figures which are considered good. These, unfortunately, whereas they present good lines as seen from the front, utterly go to pieces from a sculptural or form standpoint when viewed from the side or in profile, as they lack sufficient depth to provide good material for sideview compositions of the figure. To be sure, this *fausse maigre* type of figure often looks *chic* in clothes. But at this moment we are discussing intrinsic beauty, which is founded on the relation of parts or forms to each other, rather than a prevailing mode."[13] Even then, and all the more so by today's standards, Outerbridge's models seemed too stocky, and their limbs seemed to be too short. But the photographer primarily adopts the standpoint of a sculptor who is examining firm, compact bodies, modeling them in light, and arranging lines and masses. Following examples drawn from antiquity

zum eigenen Geschlecht und beschwört eine Feminität, die der modernen Frau abhanden gekommen sei. Vom klassischen Ideal der Venus von Milo ausgehend, beschreibt er geistreich und mit dem Auge des Connaisseurs die Beziehungen unter dem Aspekt der Proportionen des weiblichen Körpers und hebt als Hauptmerkmale dieses harmonischen Gefüges die Weichheit und die Rundungen hervor. Als Beispiel für die achtundzwanzig (!) Punkte seiner Sichtung, die, so Outerbridge, mit den achtundzwanzig Tagen der Mondphase korrespondieren, mag die Schilderung des Rumpfes oder Torsos fungieren, »der bei einem schönen Körper voll und rund sein sollte und sich vor allem durch einen tiefsitzenden Bauch auszeichnet, *ungleich* vielen amerikanischen Figuren, die als attraktiv gelten. Während sie von vorn betrachtet einen guten Kontur aufweisen, zerbricht dieser leider völlig, sieht man ihn vom bildhauerischen oder formalen Standpunkt von der Seite oder im Profil, da sie die nötige Tiefe vermissen lassen, um als gutes Material für seitliche Ansichten der Figur gelten zu können. Es ist unbestritten, daß diese *fausse maigre*-Figurtypen in Kleidung oft chic wirken. Aber im Augenblick diskutieren wir die wahre Schönheit, die sich eher auf die Verbindung der Teile oder Formen zueinander gründet als auf die vorherrschende Mode.«[13] Schon damals und um so mehr nach heutigen Standards sind Outerbridges Modelle zu gedrungen und scheinen in ihren Extremitäten zu kurz geraten. Doch der Photograph bemächtigt sich in erster Linie der Ideale des Plastikers, der feste, kompakte Körper untersucht, mit dem Licht modelliert und zum Arrangeur von Linien und Massen wird. Angeleitet von antiken Vorbildern und der Ikonographie der bildenden Künste, erarbeitet er sorgfältig Hintergründe und Accessoires seiner Kompositionen, in denen jede Pose der Modelle stimmen muß. Schon kleine Fehler machen eine stundenlang ausgefeilte Lichttechnik zunichte. Zufälligkeiten werden vom Perfektionisten Outerbridge ausgeschlossen. Bedeutende Bilder werden erdacht und gebaut, nicht mal rasch geknipst.

Der Meister selbst zieht eine schmale rigide Grenze vom künstlerischen Akt zur Pornographie, die bereits dann überschritten sei, wenn zwischen dem Modell und seinem Betrachter ein provozierendes Lächeln einen intimen Kontakt herstellte. Der Akt soll unpersönlich sein und ein möglichst universelles Konzept weiblicher Schönheit präsentieren. »Nacktheit ist ein faktischer Zustand; Unzüchtigkeit, um eine Redewendung zu erfinden, ist ein Geisteszustand.« (»Nudity is a state of fact; lewdity, to coin a phrase, is a state of mind.«[14]) Angesichts seiner Photographien argumentiert Outerbridge erstaunlich konventionell. Im Versuch, eine eigene Ästhetik zu formulieren, wird aus dem Avantgardisten

and from the iconography of the fine arts, he carefully developed the backgrounds and accessories in his compositions, into which each of the model's poses had to fit. Even minor slips could ruin a lighting technique that had taken hours to construct. A perfectionist, Outerbridge excluded all elements of chance. Important photographs are thought out and constructed, not just quickly snapped.

The master himself drew a narrow but firm line between the artistic nude and pornography, a line that had been transgressed when a provocative smile produced intimate contact between the model and her observer. The nude should be impersonal, presenting as universal as possible a conception of feminine beauty. "Nudity is a state of fact; lewdity, to coin a phrase, is a state of mind."[14] In view of the photographs he produced, Outerbridge's arguments are surprisingly conventional. In his attempt to formulate his own aesthetics, the avant-gardist became a moralizing academic whose traditional theses are belied by the modernity of his nude studies. The discrepancy between his writings and his photographic work is only explicable against the background of the conservative American society of which he, too, was a product. His nude studies are powerfully intellectualized examples of the genre, with the vividly erotic aura which they retain even today. In their realistic directness they make no attempts to deceive. Every romantic attitude is foreign to them, and they are, as a contemporary critic railed, as modern as a Bach fugue. Constructions are devised in which the observer, entering the absence of depth in their crystalline color surface, is favored with a dizzying drop into seduction, or is repelled by their glittering coolness. Outerbridge's nudes exclude any form of indifference. The nude, in the calculating act of taking a photograph, is challenging, or self-sufficient, signifies attraction or repulsion, is the reflection of the observer – and anyway, as Picabia put it, "there are no beautiful women, just as there are no truths."[15]

1 Cited after Graham Howe and Jacqueline Markham, "Von der idealen Form zum idealisierten Fetischismus," in *Paul Outerbridge Jr., Photographien 1921–1939*, Munich 1980, p. 5.
2 Ibid., p. 8.
3 Ibid., p. 15, cited from *Coronet*, March 1940, p. 25.
4 Ibid., p. 17, cited from *Information sheet on Paul Outerbridge*, ca. 1955.
5 Ibid., p. 17, cited from Paul Outerbridge, *Photographing in Color*, New York 1940, pp. 55–56.
6 Paul Valéry, *Cahiers*, Paris 1924–25, vol. 1, p. 1127.
7 Ibid., p. 1126.
8 Julia Kristeva, *Geschichten von der Liebe*, Frankfurt am Main 1989, p. 119.
9 Clement Greenberg, "Avant-Garde and Kitsch," in his *Art and Culture: Critical Essays*, Boston 1961, p. 10.

ein moralisierender Akademiker, dessen traditionelle Thesen durch die Modernität seiner Aktaufnahmen Lügen gestraft werden. Nur vor der Folie einer konservativen amerikanischen Gesellschaft, dessen Produkt auch Outerbridge gewesen ist, wird die Diskrepanz zwischen seinen Schriften und dem photographischen Œuvre erklärbar. Seine Aktaufnahmen sind in ihrer bis heute lebendigen erotischen Aura auch stark intellektualisierte Exempel des Genres. Von realistischer Direktheit, wollen sie keine Geschichten erzählen. Jegliche romantische Attitüde ist ihnen fremd, und sie sind, wie ein zeitgenössischer Kritiker polemisierte, nicht mehr Programm als eine Fuge von Bach. Konstruktionen wurden hier ersonnen, in deren Abwesenheit von Tiefe auf einer kristallinen Farboberfläche der Betrachter die Gnade des schwindelerregenden Falls in der Verführung erleben kann oder deren brillante Kälte ihn abstoßen wird. Outerbridges Akte schließen eine Indifferenz aus. Der Akt im Akt des kalkulierten Photographierens ist fordernd oder genügt sich selbst, ist Attraktion oder Repulsion, ist Widerschein des Betrachters – und überhaupt, so Picabia, »es gibt keine schönen Frauen, genauso wenig, wie es Wahrheiten gibt«[15].

1 zitiert nach Graham Howe und Jacqueline Markham, »Von der idealen Form zum idealisierten Fetischismus«, in: *Paul Outerbridge Jr., Photographien 1921–1939,* München 1980, S. 5
2 ebenda, S. 8
3 ebenda, S. 15, dort zitiert aus: *Coronet,* März 1940, S. 25
4 ebenda, S. 17, dort zitiert aus: »Informationsblatt von Paul Outerbridge«, ca. 1955
5 ebenda, S. 17, dort zitiert aus: Paul Outerbridge, *Photographing in Color,* New York 1940, S. 55 f.
6 Paul Valéry, *Cahiers,* Paris, 1924–1925, Bd. 1, S. 1127 (dt. *Cahiers/Hefte,* übers. v. Hartmut Köhler, Frankfurt/M. 1989, Bd. 3, S. 315)
7 ebenda, S. 1126 (S. 314)
8 Julia Kristeva, *Geschichten von der Liebe,* Frankfurt/M. 1989, S. 119
9 Clement Greenberg, »Avant-Garde and Kitsch«, in: ders., *Art and Culture, Critical Essays,* Boston 1961, S. 10
10 Francis Picabia, »Aphorismen«, in: ders., *Schriften, Poetische Aktion,* Hamburg 1981, Bd. 1, S. 53 f.
11 Sigmund Freud, »Fetischismus« (1927), in: ders., *Gesammelte Werke aus den Jahren 1925–1931,* Frankfurt/M. 1968[4], Bd. 14, S. 314
12 Jean Baudrillard, *Von der Verführung,* München 1992, S. 113
13 Paul Outerbridge Jr., »What is Feminine Beauty?«, in: *Physical Culture,* Januar 1933, S. 39 f.
14 Paul Outerbridge Jr., »Nude Photography in Black and White and Color«, in: *The Complete Photographer,* November 1942, H. 42, S. 2705
15 Francis Picabia, a.a.O.

10 Francis Picabia, "Aphorismen," in his *Schriften, Poetische Aktion,* Hamburg 1981, vol. 1, pp. 53–54.
11 Sigmund Freud, "Fetischismus" [1927] in his *Gesammelte Werke aus den Jahren 1925–1931,* Frankfurt am Main 1968, 4th ed., vol. 14, p. 314.
12 Jean Baudrillard, *Von der Verführung,* Munich 1992, p. 113.
13 Paul Outerbridge Jr., "What is Feminine Beauty?" in *Physical Culture,* January 1933, pp. 39–40.
14 Paul Outerbridge Jr., "Nude Photography in Black and White and Color," in *The Complete Photographer,* November 1942, issue 42, p. 2705.
15 Francis Picabia, op. cit.

1. ›Kitchen Table‹, 1921

2. ›Marmon Crankshaft‹, 1923

3. ›Telephone‹, ca. 1922

4. ›Musical-Semi-Abstraction‹, 1924/26

5. ›Waterford Glass Vase‹, 1924

6. Self-Portrait, 1927

7. ›Ten of Clubs‹, ca. 1926

8. ›Saltine Box‹, 1922/23

9. ›Ide Collar‹, 1922

10. ›Consciousness‹, ca. 1931

11. ›The Triumph of the Egg‹, 1932

12. ›Images de Deauville‹, ca. 1936

13. ›Party-Mask with Shells‹, 1936

14. Model, 1923/24

15. Standing nude with chair, ca. 1924

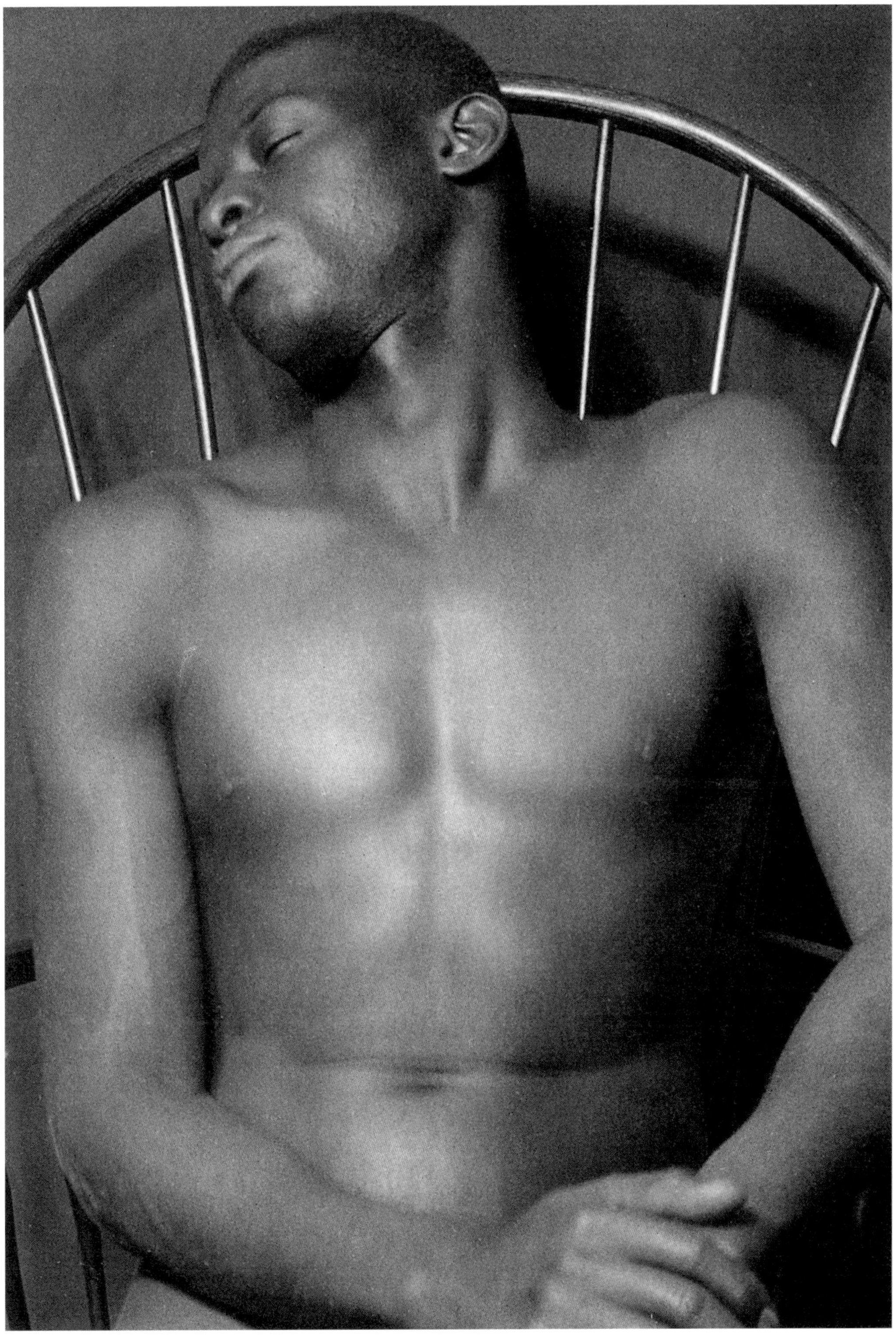

16. ›Ethiopian Form‹, 1923

17. ›Sleepy Negro‹, 1924

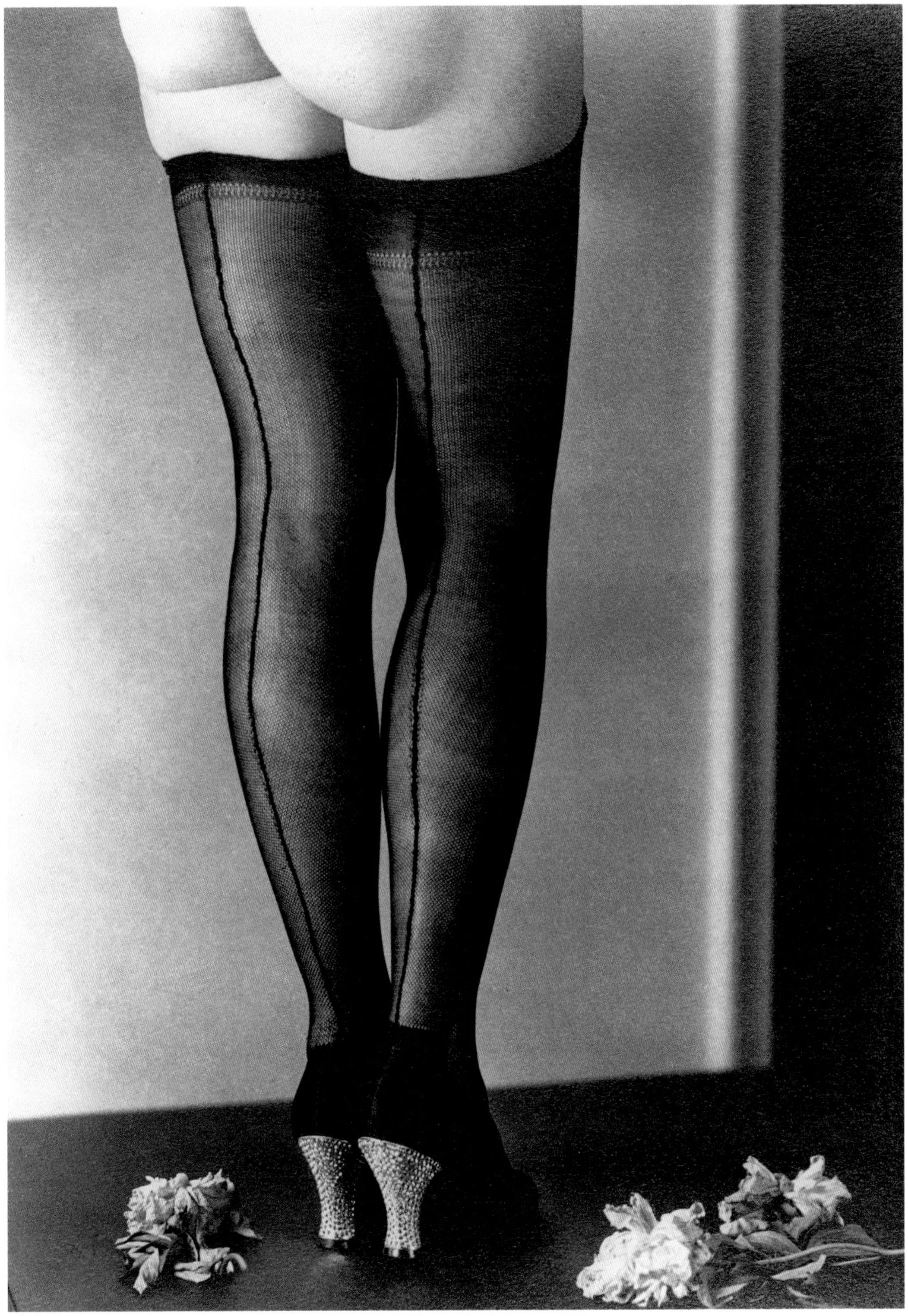

18. Legs in stockings with flowers, ca. 1928

19. Nude, ca. 1923

20. Woman in bed, ca. 1933

21. Hands and mask, ca. 1934

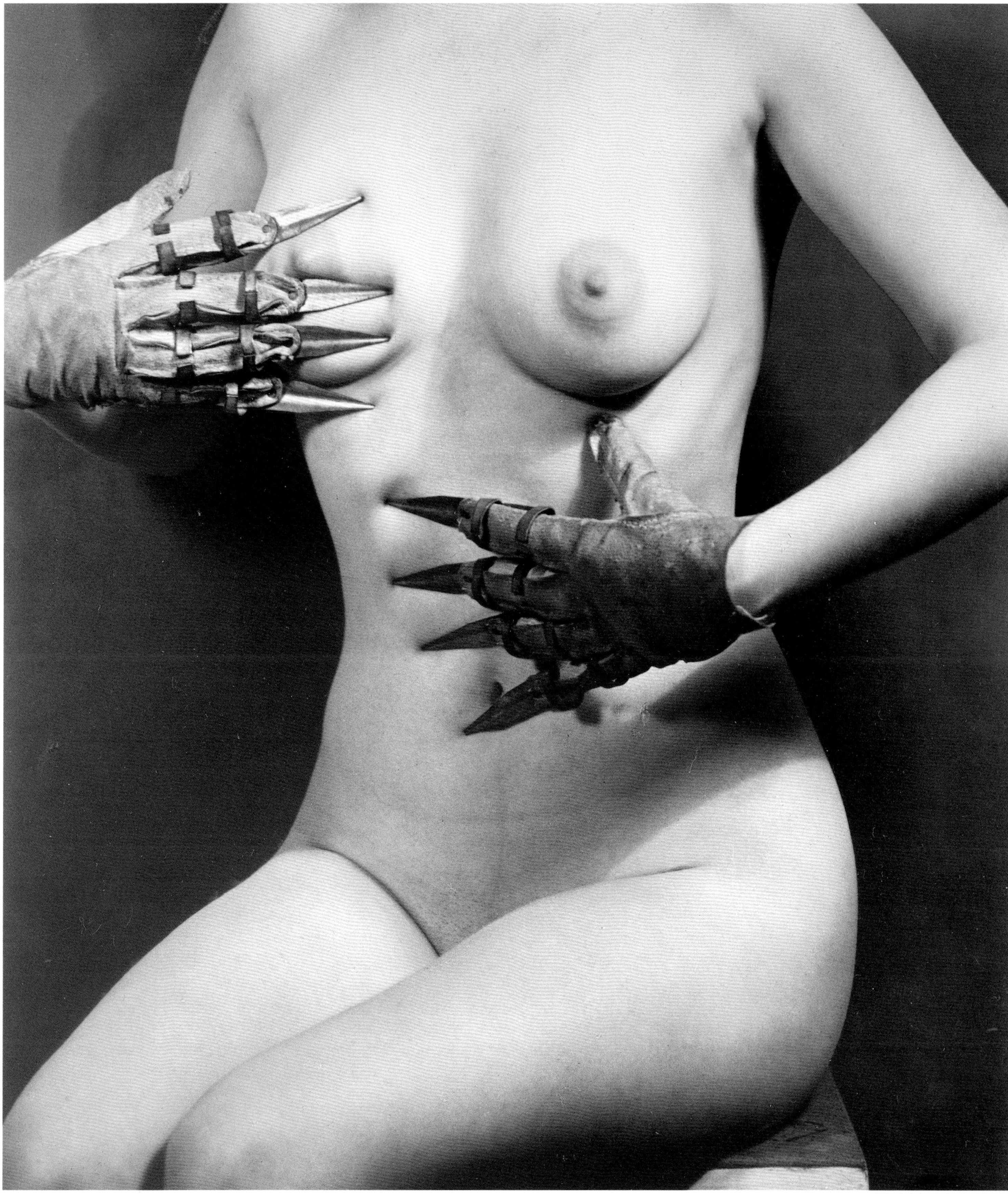

22. Woman with claws, ca. 1937

23. Nude with mask and hat, ca. 1936

24. ›Phoenix Rising‹, 1937

25. Torso, 1935/36

26. Woman with mask, ca. 1937

27. ›Shower for Mademoiselle‹, ca. 1937

28. Nude in bath, ca. 1936

29. Nude with towel, ca. 1937

30. Nude with towel, 1937/38

31. Nude lying on towel, ca. 1937

32. ›Nude with Arms Upraised‹, ca. 1938

33. Nude sitting at dressing table, ca. 1936

34. Nude with frame, rearview, 1938

35. Nude with frame, frontview, 1938

36. Reclining nude, 1937/38

37. Nude with bandleader's jacket, ca. 1936

38. ›Girl with Fan‹, ca. 1936

39. Nude lying on love seat, ca. 1936

40. Woman with snake, 1938

41. ›Dutch Girl‹, ca. 1938

42. Woman with sash and flowers, ca. 1935

43. Reclining nude, ca. 1936

44. ›Redhead‹, ca. 1937

45. Nude on ladder, 1938

46. Girl in bathing suit, 1936

47. Nude sitting, ca. 1937

Biographische Daten

1896 Am 15. August wird Paul Everard Outerbridge Junior in New York City als Sohn wohlhabender Eltern geboren.
1906 Besuch der Grundschule in New York, später der Hill School in Pottstown, Pennsylvania.
1914 Abschluß an der Cutler School in New York.
1915 Studium der Anatomie und Ästhetik an der Art Students' League in New York. Outerbridge entwirft Plakate für die *Winter Garden Revue.*
1916 Zusammen mit Rollo Peters, einem Bühnenbildner, entwirft und fertigt Outerbridge Szenenbilder. Er produziert eine eigene Revue in Bermuda und mietet ein Atelier in Greenwich Village.
1917 Outerbridge tritt als Freiwilliger in das Royal Flying Corps und später in die Armee ein.
1918 Reise nach Hollywood und Rückkehr nach New York.
1921 Heirat mit Paula Smith. Outerbridge beginnt zu photographieren. Er besucht die Clarence H. White School of Photography an der Columbia University, New York.
1922 Begegnung mit dem Photographen Alfred Stieglitz und dem Bildhauer Alexander Archipenko, der ein Studienkollege von Outerbridge ist. In der Juli-Ausgabe des Magazins *Vanity Fair* erscheint ganzseitig die Aufnahme *Kitchen Table*, im November dann die Werbeaufnahme *Ide Collar.* In den folgenden drei Jahren arbeitet Outerbridge freiberuflich als in künstlerischer Hinsicht eigenwilliger, jedoch sehr erfolgreicher Werbephotograph für die Magazine *Vogue, Vanity Fair, Harper's Bazaar* u. a.
1923 Einzelausstellung im Art Center, New York.
1925 Outerbridge geht nach Europa. Er lebt in Paris und arbeitet dort zunächst für die französische Ausgabe der *Vogue*, dann wieder freiberuflich für verschiedene Magazine. Er begegnet Man Ray, Brancusi, Picasso, Picabia, Hoyningen-Huene, Steichen, Duchamp, Strawinsky, Braque und Dalí.
1927 Gründung eines großen, aufwendig ausgestatteten Ateliers in Paris, das von dem Wachsfigurenhersteller Mason Siegal finanziell unterstützt wird, sich jedoch nicht lange halten kann.
1928 Ausstellung im »First Independent Salon of Photography«, Salon d'Escalier, in Paris. Outerbridge geht als kameratechnischer Berater zum Film, zuerst nach Berlin, dann nach London, wo er an dem UFA-Film *Varieté* mitarbeitet. In diesem Jahr wird er von seiner ersten Frau geschieden.
1929 Teilnahme an der Werkbundausstellung »Film und Foto« in Stuttgart. Rückkehr nach New York, wo er ein eigenes Studio in Monsey eröffnet und sich den neuen Möglichkeiten der Farbphotographie zuwendet. Mit seinen Farbaufnahmen im aufwendigen Carbro-Color-Verfahren ist Outerbridge in den folgenden Jahren kommerziell wieder sehr erfolgreich.
1930 Ausstellung in der American Designers Gallery in New York.
1931 Ausstellung im Albright Museum in Buffalo. Teilnahme an der »Third Annual Exhibition of Contemporary Photography«, The Ayer Galleries, Philadelphia, und an der »Eleventh Annual Exhibition of Advertising Art«, Art Center in New York.
1932 Teilnahme an der »Exhibition of Advertising Art«, Art Center, New York, und Ausstellung im Brooklyn Museum, Brooklyn, New York.
1940 Outerbridges Buch *Photographing in Color* wird veröffentlicht. Ausstellung in der Photographic Society of America Invitational Salon, Weltausstellung New York.
1943 Umzug nach Hollywood – in der vergeblichen Hoffnung, dort ins Filmgeschäft einsteigen zu können – und anschließend nach Laguna Beach, Kalifornien, wo er ein kleines Portrait-Atelier eröffnet.
1944 Teilnahme an der »Third National Print and Drawing Exhibition«, Laguna Beach, mit drei Federzeichnungen.
1945 Er heiratet die Modedesignerin Lois Weir und wird Partner in der Produktion der *Lois-Paul-Originals* für Damenmode.
1947 Outerbridge unternimmt verschiedene Reisen, um Photoreportagen für Zeitschriften zu machen.
1950 Reise nach Südamerika.
1951 Ausstellung Los Angeles County Fair.
1954 Outerbridge schreibt als freier Mitarbeiter für das Magazin *U. S. Camera.*
1958 Paul Outerbridge stirbt am 17. Oktober an Krebs. Er hinterläßt ein photographisches Werk, das knapp 600 Aufnahmen umfaßt.

Biographical Notes

1896 Paul Everard Outerbridge is born on 15 August to a prosperous family in New York City.
1906 Attends school in New York, later Hill School in Pottstown, Pennsylvania.
1914 Graduates from Cutler School in New York.
1915 Studies anatomy and aesthetics at the Art Students' League in New York. Designs posters for the *Winter Garden Revue.*
1916 Together with Rollo Peters, a stage designer, he designs and produces stage sets. He produces his own revue in Bermuda and hires a studio in Greenwich Village.
1917 Volunteers for service with the Royal Flying Corps and later with the army.
1918 Travels to Hollywood and returns to New York.
1921 Marries Paula Smith. Begins taking photographs. Attends the Clarence H. White School of Photography at Columbia University, New York.
1922 Meets photographer Alfred Stieglitz and sculptor Alexander Archipenko, a fellow student. Outerbridge's photograph *"Kitchen Table"* appears as a full page illustration in the July edition of *Vanity Fair;* in November the advertising shot "*Ide Collar"* follows. During the following three years he works freelance as an artistically independent but highly successful advertising photographer for magazines such as *Vogue, Vanity Fair, Harper's Bazaar,* etc.
1923 Solo exhibition at the Art Center, New York.
1925 Outerbridge moves to Europe. He settles in Paris and works there initially for the French edition of *Vogue*, and later freelance for various magazines. He meets Man Ray, Brancusi, Picasso, Picabia, Hoyningen-Huene, Steichen, Duchamp, Stravinsky, Dali and Braque.
1927 Establishes a large, expensively equipped studio in Paris, with financial support from the mannequin manufacturer Mason Siegal, but the project is short-lived.
1928 Takes part in the "First Independent Salon of Photography," Salon d'Escalier, Paris. Outerbridge starts working in film as an adviser on camera technique, first in Berlin and later in London, where he works on the UFA film *Varieté*. Divorce from his first wife.
1929 Takes part in "Werkbundausstellung, Film und Foto," Stuttgart. Returns to New York, where he opens his own studio in Monsey and devotes himself to the new opportunities presented by color photography. His color shots using the time-consuming carbro-color process once again make his work a commercial success.
1930 Exhibition at the American Designers Gallery in New York.
1931 Exhibitions at the Albright Museum in Buffalo, Third Annual Exhibition of Contemporary Photography, The Ayer Galleries, Philadelphia, Eleventh Annual Exhibition of Advertising Art, Art Center in New York.
1932 Takes part in the Exhibition of Advertising Art, Art Center, New York and exhibits at the Brooklyn Museum, Brooklyn, New York.
1940 Publishes his book, *Photographing in Color.* Takes part in the exhibition at the Photographic Society of America Invitational Salon, New York World's Fair.
1943 Moves to Hollywood in the vain hope of being able to enter the film business, and then to Laguna Beach, California, where he opens a small portrait studio.
1944 Three pen drawings by Outerbridge are shown at the Third National Print and Drawing Exhibition, Laguna Beach.
1945 Marries Lois Weir and becomes partner in producing the "Lois-Paul Originals" for ladies' fashion.
1947 Travels widely in connection with photojournalism projects for magazines.
1950 Travels to South America.
1951 Exhibition at the Los Angeles County Fair, Los Angeles.
1954 Writes for the magazine *U.S Camera* on a freelance basis.
1958 Paul Outerbridge dies of cancer on 17 October. His legacy is a photographic oeuvre consisting of almost 600 individual works.